ABOUT U:
A JOURNEY TO SELF

ELOIS CYSTER

Published by Legacy Design

Cape Town, South Africa

www.legacydesign

please contact preston@legacydesign.co.za or

whatsapp +27765068200

Legacy Design is committed to inspiring and equipping individuals and organizations through creative publishing, visual storytelling, and intentional design.

ISBN: 978-1-0492-1065-0

Printed in South Africa
First Edition

To my children — you have grown alongside me.
As much as I have raised you, you have also raised me.
In some ways, I am deeply sorry. In others, I am humbled and
honored to have been called "Mummy."
You are my greatest teachers. This is for you.

ACKNOWLEDGEMENT

To everyone I've ever had the privilege of encountering—thank you. Every connection, every conversation, and every moment has shaped me.

To my husband: Thank you for working tirelessly by my side and for standing with me through the not-so-happy moments, with love and strength.

To my extended family: Mum, Dad, and my siblings—I love you all. Thank you for being my roots.

And to you, my reader: Welcome. This book offers a glimpse into my world, and I hope that with each step, you feel a little closer to discovering yourself.

Because this journey isn't just mine—it's *About U*.

AUTHORS NOTE

There was a time I didn't recognize myself—not because I was lost, but because I had buried the truest parts of me beneath expectations, responsibilities, and survival.

Writing *About U* has been a journey of unearthing—of remembering the version of me that existed before the world told me who I should be. It's a mirror, a soft place to land, a quiet reminder that self-love isn't something you earn—it's something you come home to.

This book is not a manual. It's a conversation. A companion. A space where you're invited to slow down, breathe, and meet yourself again.

So, wherever you are—raw, rising, or rediscovering—I hope these words reach the deepest part of you: the part that already knows… you are worthy, whole, and enough.

With love and grace,
Elois

INDEX

INTRODUCTION

Because the most important story you'll ever tell is the one you tell yourself.

There was a moment—maybe quiet, maybe chaotic—when I realized I had spent so much of my life trying to be what the world expected that I had forgotten how to simply be me. Not the polished version. Not the people-pleaser. Not the survivor, the achiever, or the fixer. Just me. Raw. Soft. Whole.

This book is for that version of you—
The one who's tired of shrinking.
The one who's been stitched together with expectations, apologies, and armor.
The one who's ready to come home.

About U is not a manual—it's a mirror. A safe space. A conversation between souls. I'm not here to tell you who you should be. I'm simply here to remind you of who you already are—and how worthy, powerful, and lovable that person is.

Self-love isn't always bubble baths and affirmations (though those have their place). Sometimes, it's messy. Sometimes, it's choosing silence over performance. Sometimes, it's crying in your car and still showing up for yourself. It's boundaries. It's rest. It's truth.

As you move through these pages, I invite you to take what resonates and leave the rest. This is your journey—your unfolding.

This is *About U.*
Welcome home.

CHAPTER 1

Who told U that U Weren't Enough?

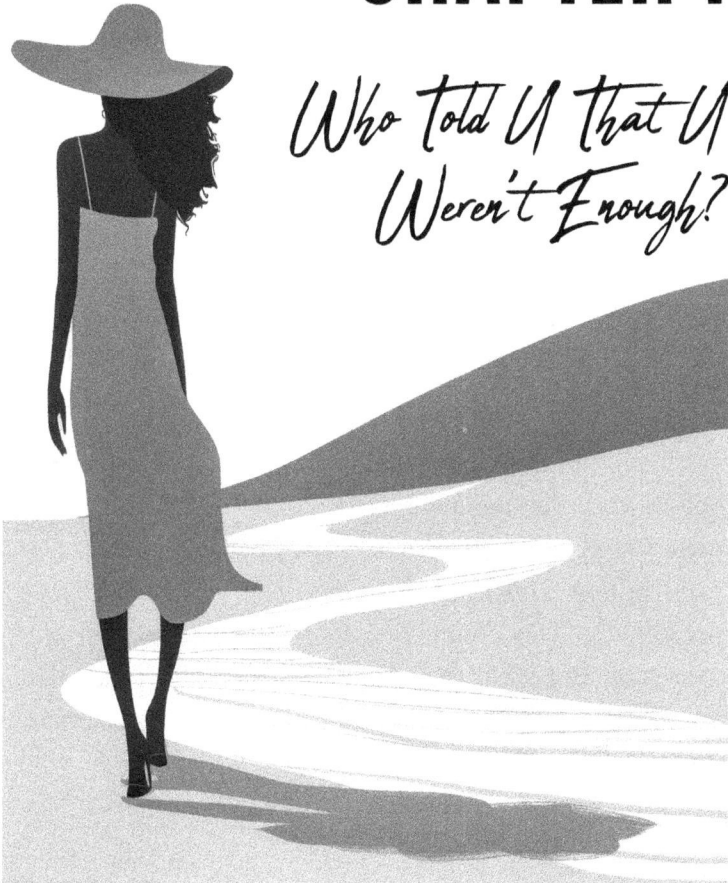

Before we can talk about loving ourselves, we must talk about the voices that convinced us not to.

They don't always scream. Sometimes, they whisper. Sometimes, they sound like a parent, a teacher, or a friend. And sometimes, they sound like you—the version of you that internalized the pain and wore it like a second skin.

This chapter is about naming those voices—not to give them power, but to take your power back.

The Moment It Started

Can you remember when you first started doubting yourself? Maybe it wasn't one single moment, but a slow drip—the look someone gave you when you were too loud, too sensitive, or too ambitious. Maybe it was an offhand comment that stuck longer than it should have. Or perhaps it was the praise that only came when you performed or pleased others.

We begin building our identity with borrowed bricks. And before long, the home we live in doesn't even feel like our own. I remember a time when I was constantly told: *Don't run like that. Don't walk like that. Don't talk like that. It's not ladylike.* Tiny comments. Subtle corrections. *Harmless*, they said. But what they really did was chip away at the essence of who I was—before I even had a chance to figure it out for myself, before I even knew who I was or who I had the potential to become.

Those small things—we often dismiss them, laugh them off, or tuck them away. But those small things become the seeds of our limitations. They form the walls that box us in long before we ever learn how to stretch our wings.

Growing up was difficult. I lived in a time when apartheid was still very much a part of everyday life. My parents, who were always loving and protective, did what they thought was best for me. Out of fear and care, they taught me how to stay safe, how to be the right kind of person in a world that wasn't kind to people like us. They showed me how to stay out of sight, how to keep my voice quiet, and how to fit in—even if it meant suppressing parts of myself. It was their way of helping me survive.

But for me, it felt like slow suffocation. I just wanted to be free. I longed to run without judgment, to speak without fear, to be bold without being labelled. But freedom wasn't made for people like us. We were taught that silence was safety, smallness was protection, and obedience was love.

All this conditioning—of who to be and who not to be—starts affecting you before you even understand it. As a developing child, it makes you constantly seek affection. You crave acknowledgment. You need validation. You begin to believe your worth is tied to how well you follow the rules, how neatly you fit the mold, how much praise you receive from the ones you're trying so hard to please. And when that becomes your pattern, the consequences echo for years.

You grow up never learning to love yourself for yourself. You become a woman who questions her every move, wondering, *Will they approve? Will they be proud of me? Am I enough?* You end up living for applause instead of joy. You perform rather than simply be.

But now I know. I see it. And I know it's time to unlearn the lie—the lie that says we are too much. The lie that says we must shrink ourselves. The lie that tells us our voices are dangerous, our dreams are too big, and our presence must be polite.

We have evolved. The world is not the same. And we no longer need to play small to stay safe. Now, we must take up space. Speak louder. Walk bolder. Live freer. It's hard to unlearn—I won't lie. It's a fight every single day. But it starts with one brave choice at a time. One belief challenged. One boundary redrawn. It starts with remembering who you were before the world told you who you should be. It starts with *you*.

Unlearning the Lie

The biggest lie you were ever told is that you had to *earn* your worth—that you had to *do* in order to *be enough*. But you were born enough. Before the grades. Before the approval. Before the wounds. This chapter is about peeling back those layers.

Ask yourself gently: *Whose voice do I still carry? What belief about myself no longer feels true, even if it once did?*

*If I could return to the moment I first felt "not enough,"
what would I say to that version of me?*

The truth is—you were never the problem. The problem
was the lens. The expectations. The projections. The truth
is: You are allowed to exist as you are, not as you "should"
be.

This book will walk you back to yourself. But for now,
pause. Breathe. You've already taken the hardest step—
asking the question.

Now, let's rewrite the answer.

Journal Prompt:
Who first made you question your enoughness? What did
they say—or what didn't they say—that shaped your self-
belief? Now, write a letter to your younger self from the
voice of love and truth.
Tell them what they need to hear.

_____

_____

_____

_____

_____

19

_____

_____

_____

_____

_____

_____

_____

_____

_____

_____

_____

_____

Affirmation:
I am not what they said I was. I am more. I am whole. I am enough, exactly as I am.

CHAPTER 2

the Masks We Wear

We're taught early on that some parts of us are lovable, and others… not so much. So we adapt. We become who we need to be to feel safe, accepted, and praised. We wear masks—*The Good One. The Quiet One. The Strong One. The Funny One. The One Who Has It All Together.*

These masks may have protected us once, but now, they're just heavy. And they're hiding the very soul we're trying to rediscover.

Why We Wear Them

Most of us never choose our masks consciously. They form out of necessity. Maybe you learned that your anger wasn't welcome, so you became agreeable. Or your softness was seen as weakness, so you became tough. Somewhere along the way, the mask became so familiar that you forgot it wasn't you. But here's the truth: anything you have to perform in order to be loved isn't love—it's approval. And approval is conditional. Self-love is not.

Taking the Mask Off

The journey of self-discovery isn't about becoming something new. It's about *unbecoming* everything you had to be to survive. We start by asking ourselves: *Who do I pretend to be when I'm around certain people? Why? What part of myself do I hide or downplay most often? If no one were watching, how would I show up?*

It's okay if you don't have the answers right away. This is tender work. Be patient with your layers. They formed for a reason—but they don't have to stay.

Permission to Be You

This chapter is your permission slip. You don't have to earn your place in the world by being "good," or "likable," or "perfect." You just have to be *real*. Because the real you—the one under the mask—is where the magic lives.

Journal Prompt:

What masks have you worn to feel safe or accepted?
Who are you when you're alone, unfiltered, and free?

_____

_____

_____

_____

_____

_____

_____

_____

_____

_____

_____

_____

_____

_____

_____

_____

_____

_____

Affirmation:
I release the need to perform. My truth is enough. My presence is enough. I am enough.

CHAPTER 3

Comparison, the Silent Thief

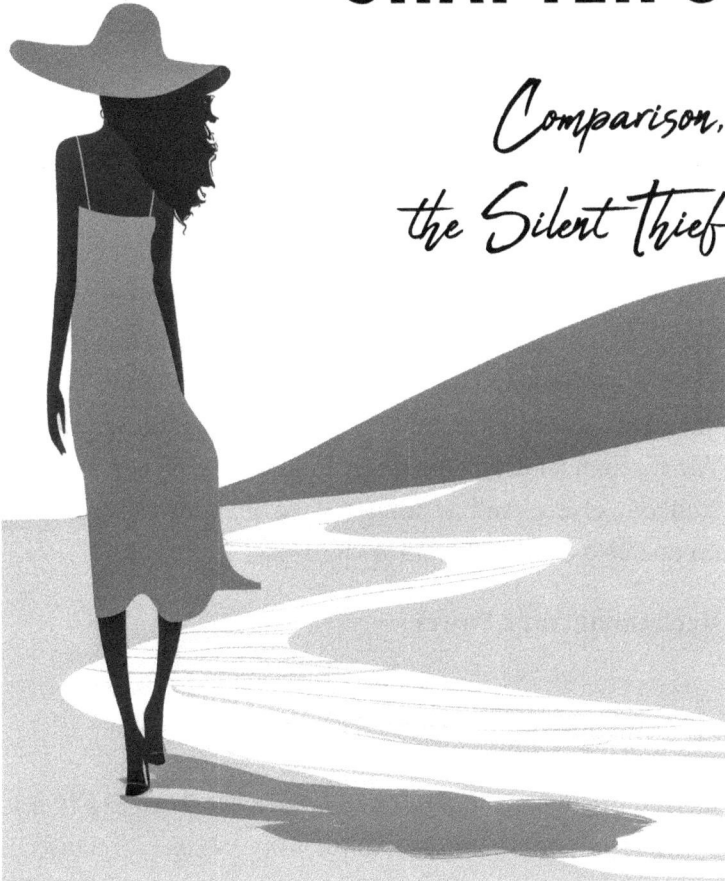

Comparison is a slow erosion.

It doesn't always shout. Sometimes it sneaks in—when you scroll through curated lives, when someone praises another and your inner voice whispers, *"Why not me?"* When their joy feels like proof of your lack.

Comparison turns self-love into a competition. And the truth is: you were never meant to compete—you were meant to *be.*

The Illusion of "Enough"

Social media, society, and even our own families often hand us a false idea of success—expectations of being more polished, more productive, more like *them.*

But here's what no one tells you: you only ever see the highlight reel, not the healing. The results are displayed, but not the hard road. The filtered smiles are evident, but not the silent, sleepless nights. When we compare, we shrink. We disconnect from our own light while trying to chase someone else's. And in doing so, we abandon the one thing no one else can offer—our *own* magic.

Reclaiming Your Power

Let's flip the script.

Instead of asking, *"Why don't I have what they have?"* ask, *"What's already beautiful about where I am?"* Instead of thinking, *"They're better than me,"* affirm, *"Their success shows what's possible for all of us—including me."*

This isn't about blind positivity. It's about remembering that someone else's shine doesn't dim your own. There's room for you too. Always.

Anchor in Authenticity
The antidote to comparison is connection—starting with yourself.

Your path isn't supposed to look like anyone else's. You were built for something uniquely yours. So bless their journey—and then root deeply into your own.

Journal Prompt:
Where in your life have you been comparing yourself the most? What has it cost you? What can you choose to celebrate about your path instead?

_____

_____

_____

_____

_____

27

_____

_____

_____

_____

_____

_____

_____

_____

_____

_____

_____

Affirmation:
There is no competition in wholeness. I honor my pace, my path, and my power.

CHAPTER 4

The Stories We Inherited

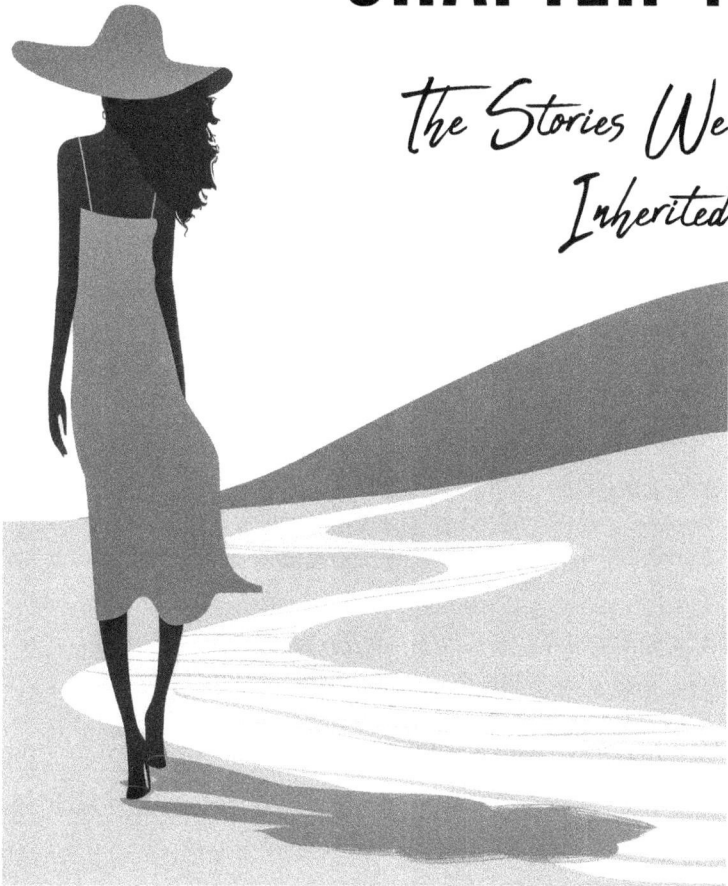

Before you were old enough to choose who you wanted to be, someone handed you a script—a story, a set of beliefs dressed as truth. Maybe it came from your family:
"Success looks like this."
"People like us don't do that."
"Love must be earned."

Or maybe it came from culture, religion, gender roles, trauma, or systems. These stories may have shaped you, but they don't own you.

What You Were Told vs. What's True

Sometimes, the things we believe about ourselves aren't ours at all. They're hand-me-downs passed through generations. They're projections from people still battling their own wounds. And here's the truth: you have the right to question everything. You have the right to rewrite the narrative—because what you believe about yourself becomes how you treat yourself.

Breaking the Cycle

To break free, you must become aware. Ask yourself: *What stories about love, success, or worth did I grow up with? Which ones still feel true—and which ones are ready to go? Who might've passed them on to me, and why?*

This work isn't about blame. It's about liberation—about realizing that healing yourself heals the line that came before you and the one that comes after.

You Get to Choose Now

You are not your past. You are not your parents' pain. You are not the rules that kept your ancestors small just to survive.

You are the storyteller now. And you get to write a story that feels like home.

Journal Prompt:

What's one story about who you "should" be that no longer fits? What new truth do you want to replace it with?

_____

_____

_____

_____

_____

_____

_____

_____

_____

Affirmation:
I release what was never mine to carry. I choose a new story—one rooted in truth, freedom, and love.

CHAPTER 5

Meeting the Mirror

There's someone you've been avoiding. Someone whose eyes hold the truth. Someone who's been waiting for your attention, your tenderness, your love.

That someone is you.

Self-love doesn't begin with fixing. It begins with seeing— really seeing. Without filters, without performance, without apology.

The Mirror Doesn't Lie, But It Can Heal

Most of us were taught to pick ourselves apart. To look in the mirror and see flaws, not features. To critique instead of connect.

But the mirror isn't your enemy—it's an invitation. An invitation to look past the layers. To sit with the version of you that's been hiding behind strength, humor, or silence.

Meeting the Mirror

I was at a retreat once with my youngest son, just before his First Holy Communion. After a short tea break, we re-entered the room, and there, on the table in front of each parent, was a mirror. We were instructed to look into the mirror and truly see the person looking back at us. To hold our own gaze. To look deeply into our eyes and feel the emotions that came up. Then, we were to journal what we felt.

But I couldn't write—because in that moment, I cried.

Tears streamed down my face as I looked at the woman in the mirror. Tired. Worried. Betrayed. Hurting. She looked lost. And she was. I was.

I had just gone through a divorce. I was raising four children. I was working a high-pressure corporate job. And in that moment, I felt like I had disappointed everyone around me—including myself. I felt unloved. Unseen. Unworthy. Every day felt like a battle to survive, and staying in the game was taxing on my soul.

And I just wanted someone to come and save me.

But I knew no one was coming.

There was no rescue party on its way. No one was going to pick me up from the floor. I had to do that myself.

In that moment of vulnerability, of hurt and stillness, I made a decision. If I couldn't do it for me yet, I would do it for my children. I would do better. I would be better. Even if I didn't know how, I would try. Because I deserved more than this survival, more than the chaos that had become my life—more than the constant disappointment and the fear of not being enough or being authentic.

That day changed me. It was the catalyst. Because I finally understood something powerful: no one is coming to save me. *I* am coming to save me.

I am worthy of me.

It started with the small things—like a simple "no" (without explanation), or "I can't right now," or "I'm busy," even if I was just planning a 30-minute shower to cry my eyes out. I *was* busy—busy working on the biggest, most important project I would ever have in this lifetime: *me.*

And now, when I look in the mirror, I smile. And she smiles back at me. I say, *Hello, you pretty princess,* and she acknowledges that back to me. I always say, *I love the human being that you are. I love the woman you've become.*

Meeting the Mirror to Meet Yourself

The purpose of meeting the mirror is to meet yourself. It's to meet yourself exactly where you are, in this moment. It's not about who you were, or who you think you *should* be—it's about seeing yourself as you truly are, right now.

In that moment, when you look in the mirror, your truth becomes clear. It's just you. No masks. No expectations. No performance. The questions you ask yourself in that mirror are the ones that will propel you forward. They will become the catalyst for change.

To be better. To do better.

Even when you've reached that "Pretty Princess" moment— when you arrive for your mirror appointment and your eyes lock—you will ask, *How can I be better today?* And the answer will come through as, *Just be you.* And that is enough.

Looking into that mirror is connecting with your higher self. In that moment, any question you have will be answered instantly. In the quiet of your own mind, you'll know what you need to do. You'll know what you need to heal, what you need to let go of, and what you need to embrace.

Meeting the mirror is extremely important. It's not just about looking—it's about *seeing*. It's about taking time for yourself, reflecting, and giving yourself the space to grow. It's a moment of self-work, a moment of truth, and a moment of deep self-love.

And that is where real growth begins. That is where the journey of self begins. This is where you will learn how to be kind to yourself.

Facing Yourself Gently

When you meet yourself in the mirror, do it with grace.

Try this: look into your own eyes. Not at your outfit, your skin, or your expression. Just your eyes. Say something kind out loud—even if it feels awkward. Especially if it feels awkward. Thank yourself. For surviving. For showing up. For trying.

It's not vanity—it's about presence. It's about reminding yourself: *"I see you. I love you. I'm not leaving you."*

What the Mirror Reflects Back

When you begin to meet yourself with love, something

shifts. You stop chasing external validation. You stop needing others to tell you who you are.

Because now—you know.

The mirror becomes a witness to your growth. A partner in your healing. A sacred space where the most important relationship of your life can bloom: the one with *you*.

Journal Prompt:

What comes up for you when you look at yourself in the mirror? What do you want to start seeing instead? How can you begin showing up for yourself with more presence and softness?

_____

_____

_____

_____

_____

_____

Affirmation:
I see myself. I honor myself. I am safe with myself.

CHAPTER 6

Feel to Heal

We've been taught that emotions are something to fix or escape. We're told to move on or get over it. But what if the way forward isn't about avoidance—it's about feeling?

Healing begins with the body.
It begins with the heart.
It begins with feeling *everything*—without judgment, without rushing to make it better.

The Power of Emotions

Emotions are messengers. They're not signs of weakness—they're signals that something inside needs attention, understanding, and love.

When you suppress your feelings, you suppress your healing. You push down the very things that want to be released. But when you allow yourself to feel, you open the door to release, transformation, and peace.

Permission to Feel

Here's a simple truth:
You are allowed to feel whatever you feel—without explanation, without shame.

Maybe you're angry.
Maybe you're sad.
Maybe you're confused, anxious, or joyful.

Whatever you feel, feel it fully. Don't rush to change it. Don't hide it. Just sit with it, breathe into it, and let it move through you.

Trusting Your Emotional Journey

Healing is not linear. Some days, you'll feel like you've made progress. Other days, you'll feel like you've taken steps back.

That's okay. That's normal.
Feel what's here today, and trust that every emotion—every tear, every laugh—is part of your growth.

The more you allow yourself to feel, the more you learn that your emotions are not your enemy. They're your teachers. And they will guide you back to wholeness.

Journal Prompt:

What emotions have you been avoiding?
How can you begin to create space to feel them without judgment or resistance?

_____

_____

_____

_____

_____

41

_____

_____

_____

_____

_____

_____

_____

_____

_____

_____

_____

Affirmation:
I honor my emotions as my teachers. I trust my feelings as part of my healing.

CHAPTER 7

The Power of "No"

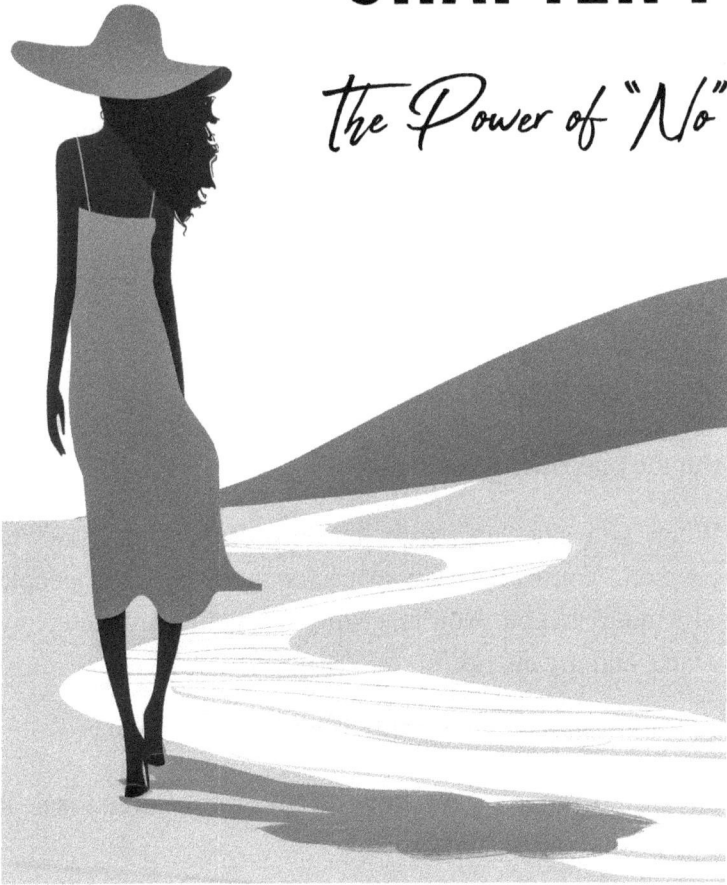

Saying "no" is one of the most loving things you can do for yourself. It's an act of self-preservation, a declaration that your needs matter just as much as everyone else's.

Yet we often resist it.
We fear disappointing people.
We fear being labeled selfish.
We fear the discomfort that comes with setting a boundary.

But here's the truth: boundaries aren't walls—they're doorways to a life that honors you. They're the space between your energy and the world around you, and they allow you to show up as your fullest, most authentic self.

The Fear of Saying No

The fear of saying no often comes from a deep-rooted belief:
If I say no, I won't be loved.
If I say no, I'll be rejected.

But the opposite is true.

When you say "no" with love, you're saying "yes" to yourself. You're creating space for the things and people who nourish you. You're saying, "I value my time, my peace, and my energy."

Learning to Say No

Saying no doesn't have to be harsh or confrontational. It can be kind, clear, and firm.

Try this: Next time you're asked to do something that doesn't feel aligned, pause. Say, "I can't right now," or "This isn't the right fit for me."
Honor your inner voice, and trust that the right opportunities will still come to you.

It's also important to remember that no is a complete sentence. You don't need to explain, justify, or apologize for taking care of yourself.

The Freedom of Boundaries

When you start saying "no" to what drains you, you create space for what energizes you. When you say "no" to things that don't align with your values, you make room for the things that matter most.

Your time, energy, and peace are precious—and they are yours to protect. Boundaries are not selfish. They are acts of self-respect.

Journal Prompt:

Where in your life have you been saying yes when you meant to say no? What is one boundary you can set today to protect your energy and peace?

_____

_____

_____

_____

_____

_____

_____

_____

_____

_____

_____

Affirmation:
Saying no is an act of love. I trust that my boundaries protect my peace, and I honor my needs.

CHAPTER 8

Rest as Resistance

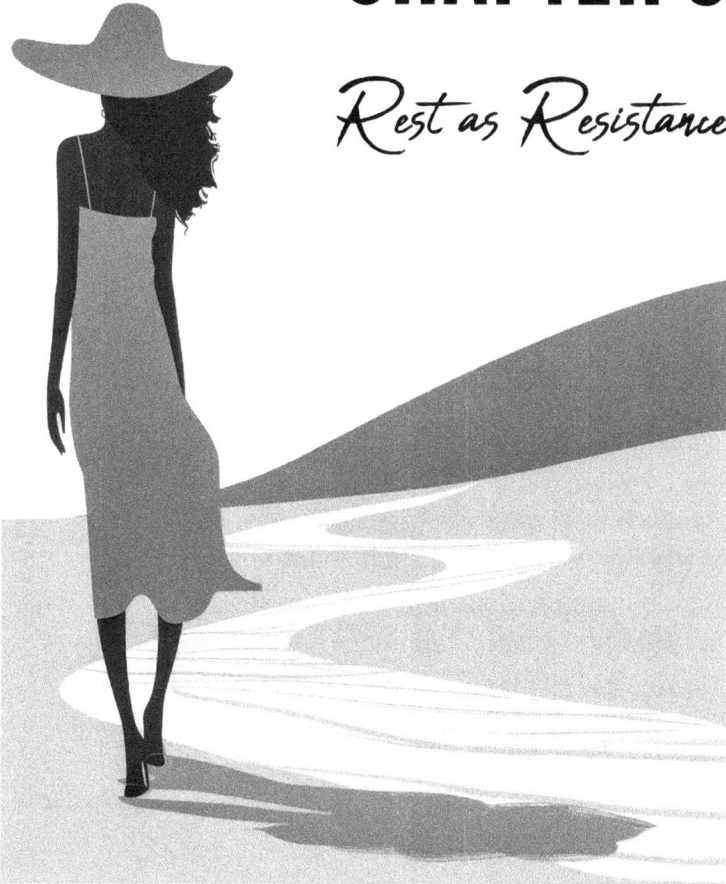

We live in a world that glorifies hustle. Where exhaustion is worn like a badge of honor, and rest is seen as laziness. But here's the truth: rest is not a luxury. Rest is a rebellion.

Choosing to rest in a world that profits off your burnout is an act of power. It says, "I am not a machine. I am human. I am worthy, even when I am still."

Why We Struggle to Rest

Many of us were raised to believe that our value lies in our doing—how much we produce, give, or accomplish.

So we feel guilty when we stop. We fidget when we slow down. We apologize for taking up space without performing. Because we are raised to be awake at the crack of dawn or be labelled as lazy.

But your worth isn't tied to your productivity. You don't need to earn rest—you deserve it. Always.

Redefining Rest

Rest is more than sleep.
It's stepping away from what drains you.
It's saying no without guilt.
It's silence, softness, solitude.
It's joy. It's play. It's simply being.

Ask yourself:
What does rest look like for me—not just physically, but emotionally and spiritually?

When do I feel most restored, most me?
What would it feel like to choose rest before I reach my
breaking point?

Rest Is a Radical Act

To rest is to reclaim your rhythm.
To resist the lie that you have to do more to be more.
To say, "I will not abandon myself for approval or pace."

The world doesn't need a more exhausted version of you.
It needs the rested you. The rooted you. The real you.

Journal Prompt:

What messages were you taught about rest growing up?
What kind of rest is your body, mind, or soul craving right
now?

_____

_____

_____

_____

_____

_____

_____

_____

_____

_____

_____

_____

_____

_____

_____

_____

_____

Affirmation:
Rest is my right. I honor my body's need to pause. I am enough, even when I am still.

CHAPTER 9

Loving the Parts U Hide

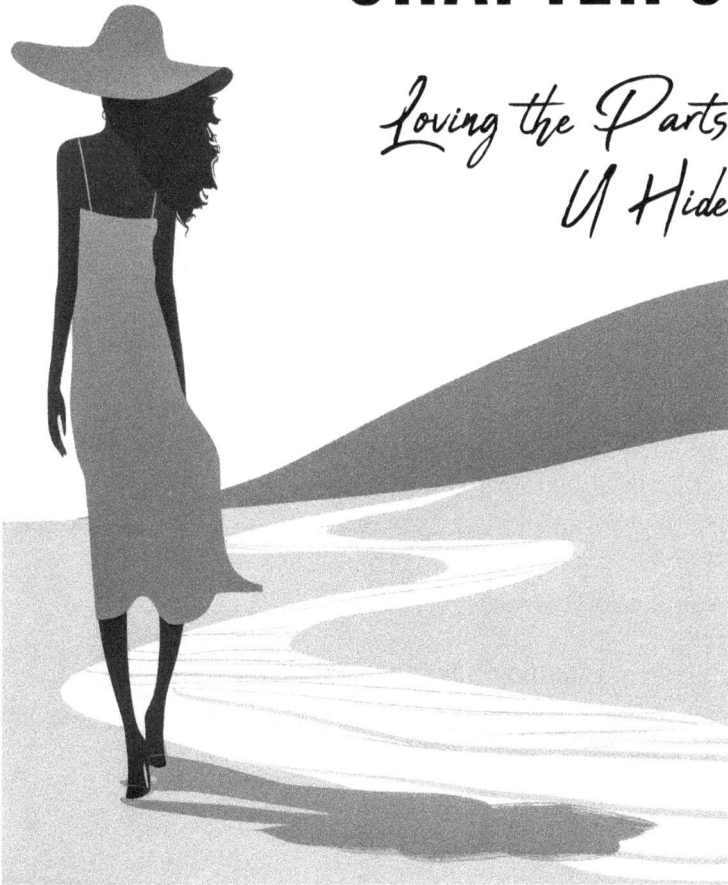

We all have parts we've tucked away.
The too-much parts.
The too-soft parts.
The awkward, angry, messy, needy, emotional parts.

We learned to hide them because we thought we had to—
To be loved.
To be accepted.
To survive.

But the truth is: the parts you hide are often the parts that need your love the most.

Where Shame Lives, Healing Waits

Shame thrives in silence. It grows in the dark corners where you've told yourself, *"I'm too much,"* or *"I'm not enough."*

But healing begins when you stop running from those places and start meeting them with gentleness.

You don't have to fix those parts. You don't have to make them prettier or more palatable. You just have to see them. Sit with them. Love them.

You Are Not Broken

What if nothing about you needs to be hidden? What if the pieces you thought made you unlovable are actually your greatest portals to connection?

Your sensitivity is not weakness—it's wisdom.
Your sadness is not a flaw—it's a signal.

Your past isn't baggage—it's part of your becoming.

Every piece of you is worthy of light.

Wholeness Over Perfection

Self-love isn't about being flawless—it's about being whole. That means embracing the light and the shadow. The joy and the jagged. The confidence and the doubt.

When you love the parts you've hidden, you begin to integrate. You become real. You become you—fully, freely, unapologetically.

Journal Prompt:

What part of yourself have you been hiding or rejecting? Why? What would it look like to love that part instead of shaming it?

_____

_____

_____

_____

_____

_____

_____

_____

_____

_____

_____

_____

_____

_____

_____

_____

_____

_____

Affirmation:
I welcome all of me. I am whole—not in spite of my hidden parts, but because of them.

CHAPTER 10

Becoming Your Own Home

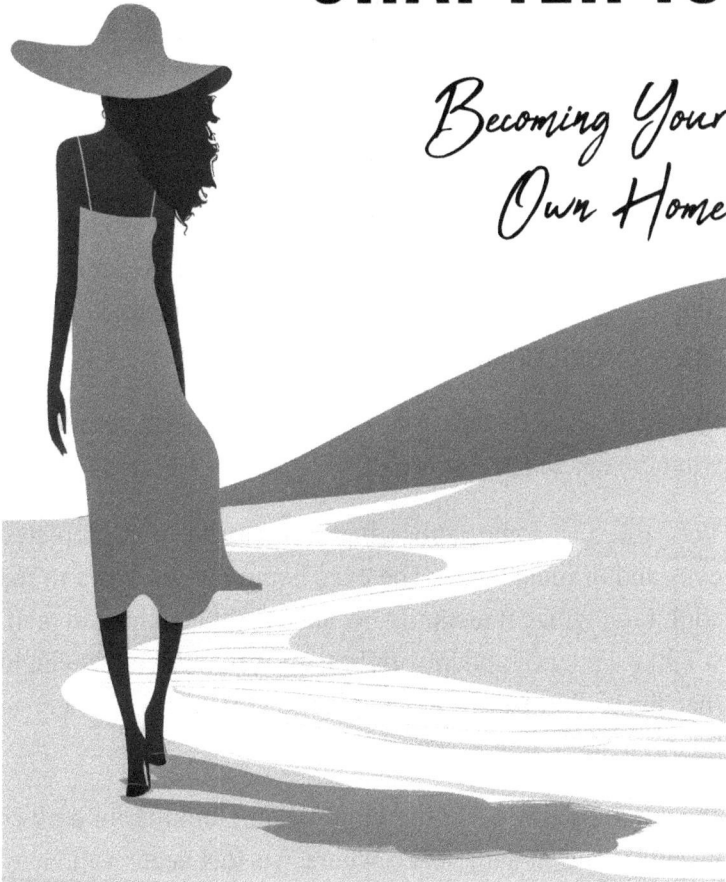

For so long, you searched for home in other people—in their validation, in their presence, and most importantly, in the way they saw you.

But true safety... true belonging... true home? That lives inside you.

Becoming your own home means learning to hold yourself gently—especially when the world doesn't. It means being the person you needed when you were hurting. It means choosing yourself, again and again, without waiting for permission.

The Loneliness of Abandonment

We often feel lonely not because no one is around, but because we've left ourselves. We've ignored our needs. Silenced our voice. Pushed away our truth to keep the peace or keep others close.

But your peace matters too. Your presence with yourself is what creates the real sense of *"I belong here."*

Very often, I come across humans, people with depleted eyes and drained souls. The eyes being the windows to the soul, I recognize it instantly because I've been there myself. It's like a silent, hidden weight they carry, and it's a weight that many don't even acknowledge until it's too heavy to bear.

We are searching for something. We are looking for a place to call home, a safe space where we feel seen, validated, and loved. And the painful truth is, many are seeking that home through someone else's eyes. They look for it in their partner's approval, in their children's affection, in the validation of the people around them.

But here's the thing: you cannot make yourself at home in someone else's validation. That will always leave you feeling empty.

No matter how much love or praise you receive from others, it will never be enough if you haven't learned to find that validation within yourself. If you haven't created a sanctuary inside yourself where you feel whole, enough, and worthy, you will always find yourself longing—constantly looking outward for something that only you can give yourself.

Becoming Your Own Home Means Loving Yourself First

You must become your own home first. You must learn to look into your own eyes, to accept your flaws, to nurture your spirit, and to love yourself unconditionally before you can truly thrive in any relationship.

When you find yourself in a relationship, marriage, or long-term commitment, and you catch yourself repeatedly operating out of fear—fear of losing someone, fear of disappointing them, fear of being unworthy unless you please them—ask yourself: *Does this person validate who I am?*

Because if that's the case, you've lost the plot.

You are valid enough on your own.

It is not someone else's responsibility to give you a sense of worth. You cannot place your happiness on another person's shoulders. They do not see through your eyes. They are not you. *You* are responsible for you.

How to Come Home to You

Coming home is a practice. It's not always loud or dramatic—it's found in the quietest moments:

- Taking a breath and checking in: *"How do I feel right now?"*

- Making space for your needs without guilt

- Soothing your inner child with kindness, not criticism

- Letting your truth be enough, even if no one else claps for it

You become your own home when you stop looking for safety "out there" and start building it within.

You Are the Constant

People will come and go.
Life will shift and surprise you.
But you—your inner sanctuary—can always be the place you return to.

No matter what happens around you, there's a soft, steady voice within saying:
"I've got you."
"I'm with you."
"Welcome home."

Journal Prompt:

When have you felt most at home with yourself? What does your ideal inner home feel like—safe, honest, calm? What's one way you can create that space within today?

_____

_____

_____

_____

_____

_____

_____

_____

_____

_____

_____

_____

_____

_____

_____

_____

_____

_____

_____

Affirmation:
I am my own safe space. I come home to myself with love, again and again.

CHAPTER 11

the Reintroduction

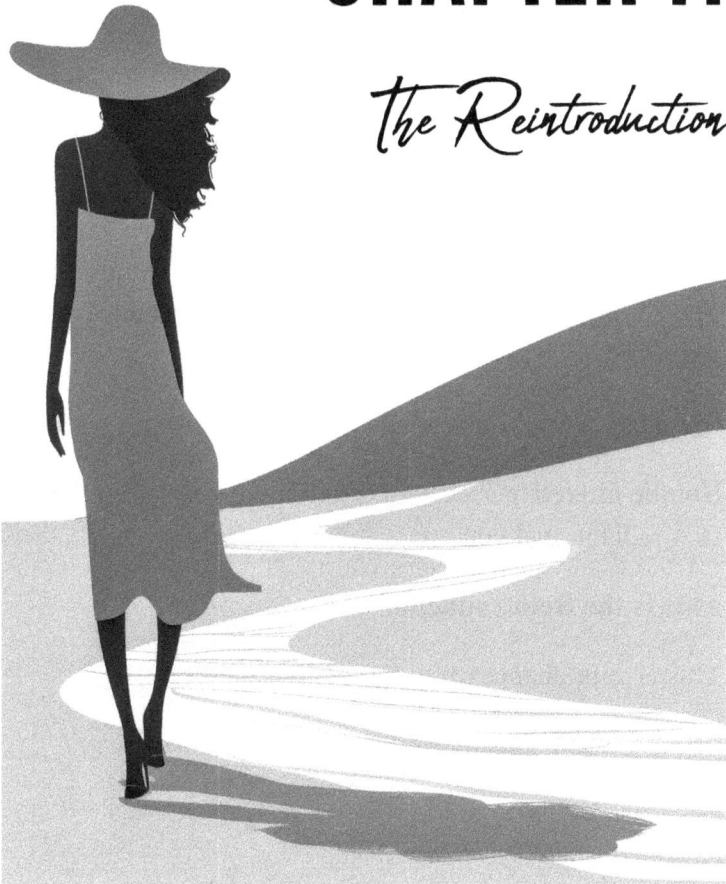

There comes a moment on the healing journey when you pause...
Look in the mirror...
And realize: *I'm not who I used to be.*

You've peeled back layers.
Released old stories.
Made room for your wholeness.

And now, it's time to meet yourself again—not as you were, but as you truly are.

Who Are You Without the Mask?

For so long, you wore versions of yourself just to belong. You were what they needed. What they expected. You dimmed your light so others could shine. You shrank your truth to fit into spaces never built for your brilliance.

But now? Now, you're ready to be seen.

Not the filtered, perfected, performative you— But the raw, radiant, real you.

This Is the Reintroduction

This is your chance to say:

"Hi, I'm [your name], and I'm learning to love who I am."

Not who you were told to be.
Not who you thought you had to be.
But who you actually are—right now. Evolving.
Expanding. Enough.

You Don't Need to Explain Your Becoming

People from your past may not recognize you anymore.
That's okay.
You didn't grow for their understanding—you grew for
your freedom.

You don't owe anyone an explanation for your healing,
your boundaries, your softness, or your power.

Let them adjust.
Let them meet you here—or let them fade.

Either way—you remain.

Journal Prompt:

If you could reintroduce yourself to the world, what would
you say? Who are you becoming, and what parts of yourself
are you reclaiming?

_____

_____

_____

_____

_____

_____

_____

_____

_____

_____

_____

Affirmation:
I reintroduce myself with pride. I am allowed to evolve, to shift, to rise—and I don't need permission to be fully me.

CHAPTER 12

U, Unapologetically

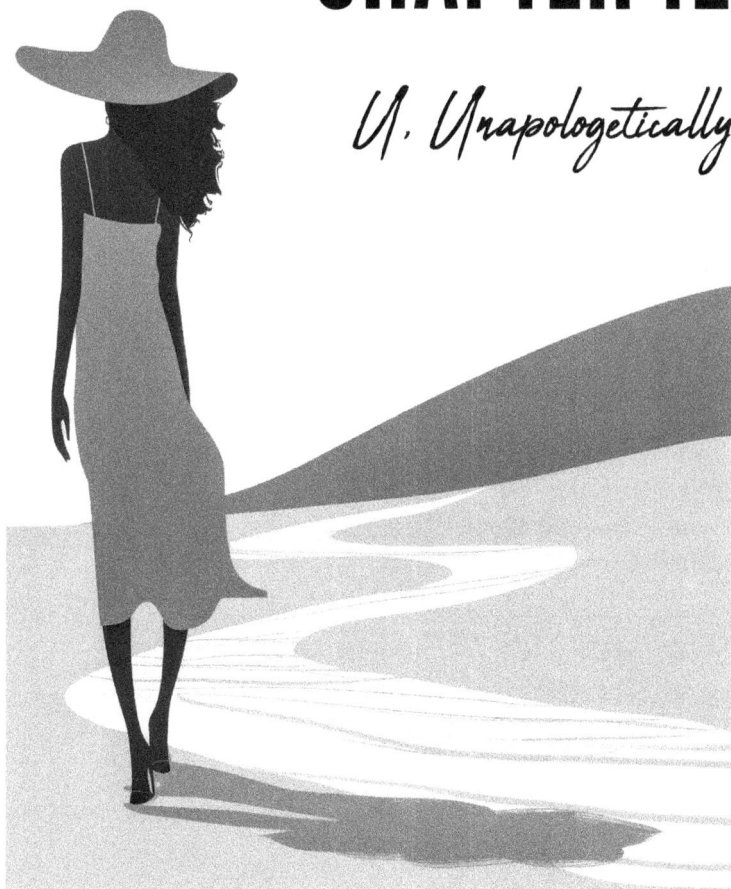

This is the moment you stop asking, *"Is it too much?"* and start saying, *"This is me—fully, wildly, beautifully me."*

You've journeyed through the ache.
Held space for the soft.
Reclaimed the hidden.

And now, you rise unapologetically.

What It Means to Be Unapologetically U

It doesn't mean being loud all the time. It doesn't mean proving yourself.

It means being true, without shrinking.
It means laughing freely, crying deeply, dreaming wildly.
It means making room for your voice in rooms that once told you to be small.
It means showing up even when you're scared—because your presence is no longer up for negotiation.

You Are Allowed To...

- Take up space

- Change your mind

- Rest without guilt

- Be soft *and* be strong

- Say no without explanation

- Choose yourself, again and again

You don't owe the world a version of you that makes them comfortable. You owe yourself the freedom to be who you really are.

This Is Not the End—it's the Beginning

You didn't come this far just to go back to who you were.
You came this far to *live*.
To thrive.
To love yourself so deeply that your very existence gives others permission to do the same.

You are proof that healing is possible.
That softness is strength.
That authenticity is power.

Being U—fully, freely, unapologetically—is more than enough. Always has been.

Journal Prompt:

What does it look like to live unapologetically as you? What are you no longer willing to shrink or silence? What promises are you making to yourself moving forward?

_____

_____

_____

_____

_____

_____

_____

_____

_____

_____

_____

Final Affirmation:
I am U. Fully. Freely. Unapologetically. And I am more than enough.

CONCLUSION

About U: Journey Back to Yourself

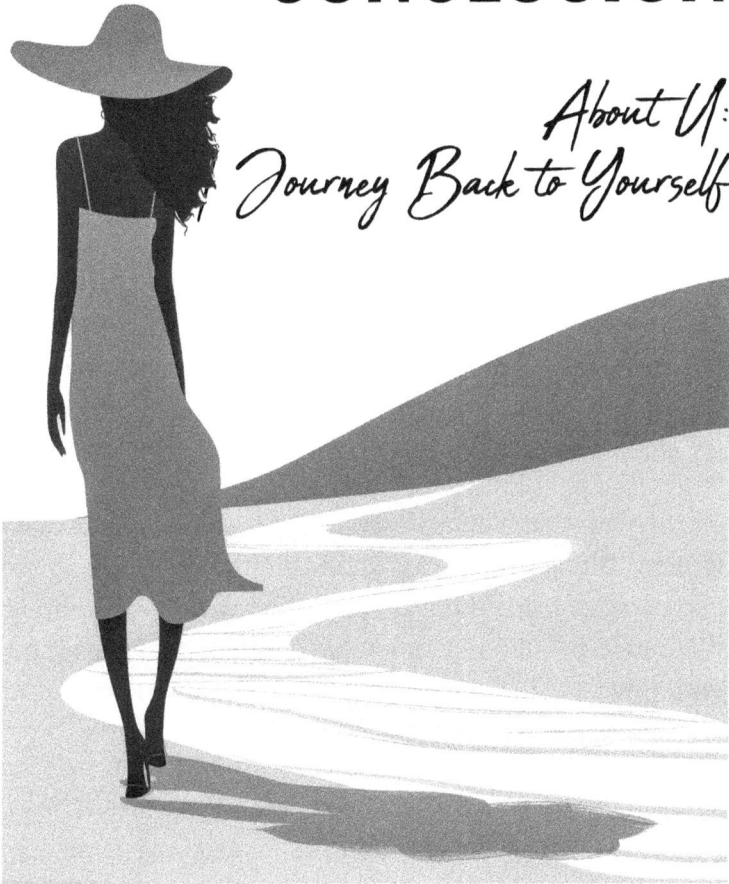

In a world that constantly asks you to be more, do more, and prove more, *About U* is a soft rebellion. A quiet, powerful invitation to stop running—and return home to yourself.

Through 12 soul-stirring chapters, Elois Cyster walks beside you on a journey of self-love and self-discovery. With raw honesty, gentle wisdom, and heartfelt journal prompts, she invites you to peel back the layers, question the myths, and meet the most important person in your life.

This isn't a book about fixing yourself. It's not a quest to change your circumstances or others. It's not about eliminating people or demanding they see your worth. *This* is about discovering what resonates with your deep, inner soul.

In a noisy world, this book invites you to silence the distractions and listen inward. The healing doesn't begin out there—it begins within. Everyone in your life is a mirror. But this journey isn't about fixing the reflections— it's about loving the source.

When you heal yourself, everything around you begins to align.It's about finding yourself. It's about loving the parts you've hidden. It's about healing what's been buried. And most of all—it's about standing unapologetically in your truth.

Whether you're in a life transition, healing from pain, or simply longing for a deeper connection with yourself, *About U* is your mirror, your permission slip, and your reminder:

You were never too much.
You were always enough.
This book is *About U*.

www.ingramcontent.com/pod-product-compliance
Lightning Source LLC
Chambersburg PA
CBHW070759050426
42452CB00012B/2413